MARIA THE CHASTE: AISHA'S ADULTERY ACCUSATION

Sheikh al-Habib

Maria the Chaste:
Aisha's Adultery Accusation

First Edition

ISBN 978 1 7385413 0 0

The Rafida Foundation
The Minor Land of Fadak
Windmill Road, Fulmer
Buckinghamshire
SL3 6HF

The Rafida Foundation
Charity no. 1182789
rafida.org

CONTENTS

I - DISCLAIMER

This book is a chapter taken from Sheikh al-Habib's book "Obscenity The Other Face of Aisha". The translator has made every effort to stay faithful to the original text, but some changes may have been made for clarity and readability.

These changes include rephrasing some parts of the text to make it easier to read and understand, replacing some Arabic phrases with more common English equivalents and shortening some sentences for clarity. Headings have additionally been added to the book to make it easier to navigate. However, the content has been subject to careful scrutiny to ensure that the meaning of the original is preserved.

II - SYNOPSIS

This abridged booklet is excerpted from Sheikh al-Habib's mighty tome "Obscenity The Other Face of Aisha". It presents information about the life of Lady Maria, the Copt, the mother of Ibrahim, son of Prophet Muhammad (peace be upon him and his pure progeny), and the vicious accusation that was made against her.

INTRODUCTION

Throughout history, Lady Maria has been unfairly overlooked. Bakri historians and biographers have repeatedly failed to acknowledge the significance of her life, despite her having lived a while after the martyrdom of the Prophet (peace be upon him and his pure progeny). They have either deliberately or unknowingly obscured the fact that the verses of the event of Ifk (i.e., imputation) were revealed to exonerate and prove her innocence.

Maria, daughter of Shamoun, was an Egyptian magnanimous and chaste young lady. As part of a gift selection, Maria was sent as a concubine in the 7th year after Hijra by Juraih Ibn Mina al-Muqawqas, the Caucasian patriarch and governor of Egypt at the time. This happened after the Prophet (peace be upon him and his pure progeny) sent him a letter inviting him to Islam. However, al-Muqawqas tenaciously feared for his authority, evasively rejected Islam, and sent selective gifts to the Prophet instead. A grizzled donkey named Ufair or Ya'four, an ashy mule named Duldul, a thousand measures of gold, twenty

Coptic garments[1] and most prominently, two young sisters were amongst the selection of gifts. Maria, whom the Prophet had chosen for himself, and Sireen, whom the Prophet gifted to his poet Hassan Ibn Thabit, who later bore him his son Abdul-Rahman. A slave named Ma'boor, or Juraih, was also sent in the gift caravan, who reportedly was either the two sisters' brother or cousin – provided there is a different opinion on his relation to the sisters.

The narrations indicate that Maria and Sireen were highly esteemed and had a noble social standing among the Copts. Aisha recognised this, as reported by Ibn Kathir:

أهدى ملك من بطارقة الروم يقال له المقوقس جارية قبطية من بنات الملوك يقال لها مارية

"One of the Roman patriarchs who was known as al-Muqawqas gifted a Coptic girl of royal descent whose name was Maria"[2].

In addition, al-Muqawqas's statement in his reply to the Holy Prophet (peace be upon him and his progeny) corroborates this fact as he is reported to have said:

وبعثت إليك بجاريتين لهما مكان في القبط عظيم

---

1 *Uyoon al-Athar by Ibn Sayid an-Nas, vol. 02, pg. 395*

2 *Al-Sira an-Nabawiyah by Ibn Kathir, vol. 04, pg. 603, on the Isnad of Abu Na'im*

"I am sending to you two young ladies who are highly regarded among the Copts"[3].

As for how the two honourable young ladies came to be enslaved by al-Muqawqas, some historical texts suggest that Maria and Sireen were, in fact, Christian monotheists adhering to the same religion of their father Shamoun, who was a fierce adversary of al-Muqawqas and most likely met his destiny in one of his bloody battles.

The sectarian divide between al-Muqawqas and the Coptic Egyptians of the time sparked intense wars between the two parties; as he sought assistance from the Roman-Byzantine Emperor Heraclius, al-Muqawqas managed to impose his power and authority over the Coptic Egyptians. He further transgressed to coerce them into adhering to a new Christian dogma. This suggests that Shamoun's objection was entirely on religious grounds and purely motivated by the concern to preserve the true religion of Jesus (peace and blessings be upon him). As a result, Maria and Sireen, after the death of their father, were taken captives and eventually enslaved by the grip of al-Muqawqas[4].

---

3 *Al-Tabaqat al-Kubra by Ibn Sa'd, vol. 01, pg. 260*

4 *In Kitab al-Fath al-Islami Li Misr by Ahmed Adil, it has been reported al-Muqawqas, the governor of Egypt, introduced a new sect of Christianity called the Chalcedonians. The Copts rejected the new sect and thus were subjected to bloody wars and sever punishment. The Copts also rejected the new patriarch appointed by al-Muqawqas to the Alexandrian church. One of the Copts who rejected him was Shamun, the father of Maria.*

THE LIGHT WITHIN

Nonetheless, Lady Maria embraced Islam before meeting the Holy Prophet (peace be upon him and his pure progeny) on her journey from Egypt to Madinah. It was Hatib Ibn Abi Balta'a who invited her to embrace the religion[5]. This illustrates the soundness of her mind and the radiance of her soul. In addition to her commitment to the faith, Maria (peace be upon her) was an appealing, beautiful, and radiant young lady. She, therefore, endowed both a striking physical merit and, most importantly, a solid moral compass. These qualities spawned a special place in the Prophet's heart for her.

---

5 *Al-Tabaqat al-Kubra by ibn Sa'd, vol. 01, pg. 260 and al-Isaba by ibn Hajr vol. 08, pg. 311*

THE PORTRAIT OF BEAUTY

كان رسول الله صلى الله عليه وسلم يُعجب بمارية القبطية، وكانت بيضاء جعدة جميلة (...) وكانت حسنة الدين

"The Messenger of Allah, peace be upon him, admired Maria the Copt. She was fair-skinned and beautiful. She had excellent observance of the religion"[6].

Consequently, the Holy Prophet's fondness for Lady Maria ignited the fire of jealousy in Aisha's spiteful and envious heart. This is expected for the one sinking in the foul filth usually envies those soaring in pristine purity. Aisha and Lady Maria (peace be upon her), in all respects, are polar opposites. Aisha was disparaged as "the horn of Satan and head of disbelief"; this is in marked contrast to Lady Maria, who was esteemed as an "excellent observer of the religion". Moreover, Aisha's low background as a granddaughter of the

---

6 *Al-Bidayah and an-Nihaya by Ibn Kathir, vol. 05, pg. 320, on the authority of al-Waqidi*

wretch of Bani Tamim does not bear a slight comparison with Lady Maria, who was the scion of Coptic kings"! Additionally, the physical features of the two are strikingly different for Aisha was dark-skinned, unsightly and constantly menstruating", whereas Lady Maria was reported to be "fair-skinned, appealing and beautiful"!

Aisha admitted to feeling jealous of Lady Maria. She is reported to have said:

ما غرتُ على امرأة إلا دون ما غرتُ على مارية، وذلك أنها كانت جميلة من النساء جعدة وأُعجب بها رسول الله صلى الله عليه وسلم، وكان أنزلها أوّل ما قَدِمَ بها في بيتٍ لحارثة بن النعمان، فكانت جارتنا، فكان رسول الله عامّة النهار والليل عندها، حتى فرغنا لها فجزعت! فحولها إلى العالية، فكان يختلف إليها هناك، فكان ذلك أشد علينا! ثم رزق الله منها الولد وحرمنا منه!

"I have never felt so jealous of a woman as I did of Maria, for she was beautiful and had sculpted facial features. The Messenger of Allah (peace be upon him) admired her. When he first brought her in, he accommodated her in the house of Harith ibn al-Nu'man, and she became our neighbour. He was with her most of the day and night. So, we malevolently made ourselves the bane of her life, and thus she became unease! He then moved her to al-'Alia', but he saw her continuously there, which became even more challenging for us to bear. Then God

blessed him with a son from her while denying us this blessing" [7].

Based on the foregoing, Aisha's jealousy grew rampant of Lady Maria because she was "beautiful" and further attained an "admirable" place in the Prophet's heart. As the Prophet's used to spend most of the day and night with her, it suggests as if he (peace be upon him and his pure family) sought respite from the constant problems, conspiracies and drama of both Aisha and Hafsa.

As Lady Maria initially moved into Harith ibn al-Nu'man's house, where Aisha and her companions also resided, she was quickly mistreated and harassed. Aisha admits: "So we malevolently made ourselves the bane of her life, causing her to feel uneasy"! This implies that Aisha's ill-treatment of Lady Maria was intended to create tension, provoke conflict, and cause problems, a dark end she was intrigued to reach to get Maria divorced eventually. This was Aisha's tactic with all the other wives of the Prophet (peace be upon him and his pure progeny), for the fire of jealousy will never die down until they are divorced.

---

7 *Al-Tabaqat by Ibn Sa'd, vol. 08, pg. 212, al-Isaba by Ibn Hajar, vol. 08, pg. 311 and other sources. In the narration reported by as-Samhoudi in Wafa al-Wafa vol. 03 pg. 826 instead of "So, we malevolently made ourselves the bane of her life" he reports: "So, we hurled at her the most foul and obscene language we could think of". This implies that the Prophet (peace be upon him and his pure progeny) moved her away to protect her from their foul tongue.*

However, despite being young, quiet, innocent, and benevolent, Maria displayed remarkable wisdom. Her piety and devolution to Allah meant that she entrusted all her matters entirely to Him. Her unwavering commitment to righteousness shone through her actions as she always made sure never to cause harm to the seal of Prophets (peace be upon him and his pure progeny). Thus, she continued to flourish in his heart.

Consequently, to provide relief, the Holy Prophet (peace be upon him and his pure progeny) relocated Maria to al-'Alia', a dwelling on the outskirts of Madinah, which was subsequently named Mashrabat Um Ibrahim, meaning Orchard of the mother of Ibrahim. It was a breathing space, although she lived in a somewhat solitary manner.

Did this eventually dispel Aisha's simmering resentment or bring her joy?! Alas, the jealousy only grew darker and more profound, like a poison coursing through her veins, due to the frequent visits made by the Prophet (peace be upon him and his pure progeny) despite the distance, which, as Aisha reports: "became even harder for us to bear". Furthermore, to crown it all, Aisha became increasingly enraged when the Holy Prophet (peace be upon him and his pure progeny) was blessed with a beloved son named Ibrahim from Maria. Despite being married for many years, neither Aisha nor any of her co-wives had been able to bear a child that could bring joy and happiness to the Prophet (peace be upon him and his pure progeny). This left Aisha feeling bitter and resentful.

Maria was the target of envy and jealousy from the other wives for her devotion to the religion of Islam, nobility, and beauty, both before and after the birth of Ibrahim (peace be upon him). However, Aisha stood out as particularly covetous, jealous, and the most envious.

As reported by ibn Saad in al-Tabaqat al-Kubra:

إن رسول الله صلى الله عليه وآله وسلم حجب مارية، وكانت قد ثقلت على نساء النبي صلى الله عليه وآله وسلم وغِرنَ عليها، ولا مثل عائشة!

"Verily the Apostle of Allah, may Allah bless him, secluded Maria, since the wives of the Prophet (peace be upon him and his pure progeny) were annoyed and jealous of her, but none as much as Aisha"! [8]

8 *Al-Tabaqat al-Kubra by Ibn Sa'd, vol. 01, pg. 135*

THE SCARS OF JEALOUSY

If Maria's beauty ignited consuming jealousy in Aisha's heart, if seeing young and beautiful Maria taken into a private accommodation of her own, cherished and protected by the Holy Prophet (peace be upon him and his pure progeny) added fuel to the fire, then finding out that Maria was pregnant only made the green-eyed monster utterly burn down!

At the first sighting of Maria's pregnancy, Aisha became restively aggravated! Ibn Kathir reported Aisha to have said:

فدخل رسول الله صلى الله عليه وسلم منها ذات يوم يدخل خلوته، فأصابها فحملتْ بإبراهيم، فلمّا استبان حملها جزعتُ من ذلك!

"The Messenger of Allah went in to see her one day when he would go to his private room and consummated with her. She

became pregnant with Ibrahim. When her pregnancy became visible, I was much aggravated".[9]

This is what Aisha is like; she casts an evil eye on the good fortune of others; envy gnaws her from within, and her blood boils with rage like a "blacksmith's forge", as described by the commander of the faithful (peace be upon him).[10]

When the light of Ibrahim (peace be upon him) shone forth to the worlds by his auspicious birth in Dhul Hijjah in the 8th year A.H., the Holy Prophet (peace be upon him and his pure progeny) was delighted and so were all the Muslims, except for Aisha. Rage pulsed through her veins, and her long-harboured hatred spiked horrid thorns! As envy does not abate, but when it is compared to the misery of others, she called into question Maria's fidelity and moral rectitude. She even went as far as to claim that Ibrahim could not be the Prophet's son claiming that he bore no resemblance to him!

Reported al-Waqidi on the authority of Urwa, narrated Aisha:

لمّا وُلِدَ إبراهيم جاء به رسول الله صلى الله عليه وسلم إليَّ، فقال: انظري إلى شبهه بي فقلتُ: ما أرى شبهاً! فقال رسول الله صلى الله عليه وسلم: ألاّ ترينَ إلى بياضه

---

9 *As-Sira an-Nabawiya by Ibn Kathir, vol. 04, pg. 603 and al-Aahad Wal Mathani by ad-Dahak, vol. 05, pg. 448*

10 *Nahj al-Balagha, quote no. 156. It means that the grudge in Aisha's heart is like a blacksmith's forge, capable of melting iron.*

ولحمه!؟ فقلتُ: إنه من قَصُرَ عليه اللّقاح ابْيَضَّ وسّمُن!
وفي رواية أخرى: مَن سُقِيَ ألبان الضأن سَمُنَ وابْيَضَّ!

"When Ibrahim was born, the Messenger of Allah brought him to me. He said: look how he bears a close resemblance to me. I said: I see no resemblance whatsoever! He exclaimed: can you not see that he is plump and fair-skinned? I said: whoever has only nourished the milk of dairy cattle [on another account, sheep's milk] will grow plump and fair"! [11]

Reported al-Hakim, on the authority of Urwa, narrated Aisha:

أُهديت مارية إلى رسول الله صلى الله عليه وآله ومعها ابن عمّ لها. قالت: فوقع عليها وَقعةً فاستمرّت حاملاً. قالت: فعزلها عند ابن عمّها. قالت: فقال أهل الإفك والزور: من حاجته إلى الولد ادّعى ولد غيره! وكانت أمةً قليلة اللّبن، فابتاعت له ضائنة لبون، فكان يُغذى بلبنها فحَسُنَ عليه لحمه. قالت عائشة رضي الله عنها: فدخل به عليَّ النبي صلى الله عليه وآله وسلم ذات يوم فقال: كيف ترَيْن؟ فقلتُ: من غُذّيَ بلحم الضأن يَحسُنُ لحمه. قال: ولا الشبه؟ قالت: فحملني ما يحمل النساء

---

11 *Al-Tabaqat al-Kubra by Ibn Sa'd, vol. 01, pg. 137 on the authority of al-Waqidi, Tarikh al-Ya'qubi, vol. 02, pg. 87*

من الغيرة أن قُلتُ: ما أرى شبهاً! قالت: وبلغ رسول الله صلى الله عليه وآله ما يقول الناس، فقال لعلي خُذ هذا السيف فانطلق فاضرب عُنُقَ ابن عمّ مارية حيث وجدتَه. قالت: فانطلق فإذا هو في حائط على نخلة يخترف رطباً، قال: فلمّا نظر إلى علي ومعه السيف استقبلته رعدة. قال: فسقطت الخرقة فإذا هو لم يخلق الله عزّ وجل له ما للرجال، شيءٌ ممسوح!

"Maria was gifted to the Messenger of Allah (peace be upon him and his pure progeny), and she was accompanied by her cousin. When she fell pregnant, the Messenger of Allah secluded her by her cousin. The people of slander and falsehood said that he claimed the child of someone else due to his need for a child. Maria had very little milk supply, so she purchased a milker ewe, and the child would be fed the ewe's milk. Due to this, he became plump and gained weight."

Aisha continues: "The Messenger of Allah (peace be upon him and his progeny) brought him to me one day. He asked: What do you think? I said: Whoever is nourished with sheep's milk becomes plump. The Messenger of Allah said: No resemblance? I was overwhelmed with the pervasive jealousy that overwhelms women, so I said: I see no resemblance.

"News reached the Messenger of Allah of what people were saying, so he instructed Ali to take the sword and cut the neck

of Maria's cousin wherever you find him. Accordingly, he proceeded and found him in an orchard on date palm plucking fresh dates. When the latter saw Ali, a shudder went down his spine, so his loin cloth fell, and Ali saw that Allah did not create for him what he created for men. It was just smooth".[12]

Reported al-Dahak and Abu Na'eem that Aisha said about Ibrahim:

فلم يكن لأمّه لبن، فاشترى (رسول الله) له ضائنةً لبوناً فغُذيَ منها الصبيّ فصَلُحَ عليه جسمه وحَسُنَ لحمه وصفا لونه، فجاء به ذات يوم يحمله على عنقه فقال: يا عائشة كيف ترينَ الشَّبَه؟ فقلتُ وأنا غَيْرى: ما أرى شبهاً! فقال: ولا اللحم!؟ فقلتُ: لعمري فمن يُغَذَّى بألبان الضأن ليحسُنُ لحمُه!

"Since his mother had a low milk supply, the Messenger of Allah bought him a milker ewe from which the boy was nourished and thus, subsequently, he exhibited a very well and healthy appearance. He (i.e., the Prophet, peace be upon him and his pure progeny) came one day holding him and said: O Aisha, how much does he resemble me? Overwhelmed with jealousy, I said impulsively: I see no resemblance! He exclaimed,

12 *Mustadrak al-Hakim, vol. 04, pg. 39*

not even the flesh! I said, by my life, whoever is nourished by the milk of ewe will look plump"![13]

13 *Al-Aahad Wal Mathani, vol. 05, pg. 448, al-Bidaya Wal Nihaya by Ibn Kathir, vol. 05, pg. 326 on the authority of Abu Na'im*

SIGNIFICANT FINDINGS

This group of narrations signify a number of findings, the key of which are:

•

- Lying through her teeth, Aisha admits that jealousy drove her to falsely deny the close resemblance between the Holy Prophet (peace be upon him and his pure progeny) and his son Ibrahim, as she says: "I was overwhelmed with the pervasive feeling of jealousy that overwhelms women; thus, I said, I see no resemblance"! Therefore, we conclude that as classified amongst the Greater Sins, lying cannot be justified in Islamic law and deemed permissible if it was out of devouring jealousy and indeed, on the Day of Judgement, one could not be pardoned for it simply because they had swollen spite!

- An analogue to the slander, Aisha's deceiving statement "I see no resemblance" was in furtherance of the slanderer's hideous claim against the Prophet "Due to his need for a child, he claimed the child of someone else". The context reveals that despite acknowledging the slander as transgressive and totally devoid of any truth, she supported it purely out of jealousy. As a result, her baneful words left a significant emotional trace on the Prophet, and thus he ordered the commander of the faithful to seek Maria's cousin.

- Aisha condemned those who had perpetrated the lie against Maria as people of grievous Ifk "imputation". This is the same condemnation used in the Holy Quran, as it says: "Verily, those who have brought forth the imputation are a group among you". The word Ifk is present in two groups of narrations, one concerning Aisha on the return from the battle of Banu Mustaliq and the other concerning Maria and her cousin. Since the narrations of Ifk concerning Aisha have been proven void, the ones relating to Lady Maria are concluded to be valid.

THE VERSE OF IFK

Based on the historical context in which the verse of Ifk was revealed, it can be logically concluded that Lady Maria was exonerated of the slanderous calumny. By examining the narrations, one can see a stark contrast between the accounts of Aisha and Lady Maria. The narrations regarding Maria are sound, faultless, and non-contradictory, while Aisha's version appears frail, contradictory, and riddled with inconsistencies.

In addition, the narrations pertaining to Maria align with the description of the woman mentioned in the Holy Quran. The verse states:

﴿إِنَّ الَّذِينَ يَرْمُونَ الْمُحْصَنَٰتِ الْغَٰفِلَٰتِ الْمُؤْمِنَٰتِ لُعِنُوا فِي
الدُّنْيَا وَالْءَاخِرَةِ وَلَهُمْ عَذَابٌ عَظِيمٌ﴾

Indeed, those who [falsely] accuse chaste, unaware, and believing women are cursed in this world and the Hereafter; and they will have a great punishment.[14]

It is evident that the virtuous characteristics of the woman portrayed in the Quranic verse are vastly different from someone like Aisha.

The claim that Aisha was a "believing woman" has been disproven by both the Quran and Sunnah. As for the assertion that she was "unaware", is incorrect as she was known to have eyes as sharp as a hawk; nothing escaped her. As for the claim that she was "chaste", then this book[15] is bound to reveal astonishing factual accounts proving the contrary. If you previously believed Aisha was chaste, then the narrations about "Adult breastfeeding", "Adorning maids", "The red dyed garment", "The green crocks", and the shameful account of "what happened on the way to Basra" will undoubtedly take you to a counter perspective.

However, as for Maria, the quality of {believing women. applies to her since, as proven, "she had excellent observance of the religion". There is absolutely no evidence in the Quran or Sunnah of her ever committing any violations or causing any harm to the Holy Prophet (peace be upon him and his pure progeny). In all senses, she was a spring of water, a source of happiness and comforting relief, a paragon of God-

---

14 *Quran 24:23*

15 *By "this book" Sheikh al-Habib is referring to the entire content of his book Obscenity The Other Face of Aisha*

consciousness and piety, and further maintained a good martial relationship with the Prophet (peace be upon him and his pure progeny) all throughout.

Maria's gentle and forbearing nature is evident in her steadfast endurance of hardship. Despite spiteful aggression, malicious slander, and vile expletives from Aisha, she did not repay evil with evil. This demonstrates unblemished piety and an immaculate inner self. Furthermore, the fact that Allah the Most Exalted bestowed her with a noble son from the Holy Honourable Prophet (peace be upon him and his pure progeny) while all the other wombs were deprived reveals that she was divinely chosen for her wholehearted and sincere faith in both her inner and outer selves.

There is no basis for the argument that Lady Maria might not fit the description of a unaware.. This is because historical evidence indicates that Lady Maria lived a secluded life on the outskirts of Madinah, refraining from idle chatter and socialising even after the martyrdom of the Holy Prophet (peace be upon him and his pure progeny). This was done in strict dutiful obedience to Allah's command to:

﴿وَقَرْنَ فِى بُيُوتِكُنَّ وَلَا تَبَرَّجْنَ تَبَرُّجَ الْجَٰهِلِيَّةِ الْأُولَىٰ﴾

And stay in your houses and do not display yourselves like that of the time of earlier ignorance.[16]

---

16 Quran 33:33

Furthermore, Maria lived among Arabs as a foreigner, being Coptic, speaking a different language and having a different cultural background. Linguistic limitations and cultural barriers often cause people to drift apart, leading to a lack of awareness due to limited social interactions.

As for her being {chaste., Lady Maria has set an admirable example of chastity, modesty, and morality, leaving a glorious legacy for future generations to follow.

It is pivotal to observe that in the very first opening of the verse of Ifk Allah The Most Exalted declares that those who concocted the slander were an "Usbah", as it says in the Quran:

﴿إِنَّ الَّذِينَ جاءوا بِالإِفكِ عُصبَةٌ مِنكُم﴾

Indeed, those who came with falsehood are an Usbah.[17]

As it has been proposed in greater detail in the seventh listed citing[18], the Quranic phrase used, "Usbah", which means a joined group of people for a shared purpose, does not apply to the people Aisha claimed had slandered her! This is because there is no historical evidence to suggest that Abdullah ibn Ubay, Hassan ibn Thabit, Mistah ibn Uthatha and Hammanah bint Jahsh were ever associated with each other. In fact, Abdullah ibn Ubay was a known hypocrite who was isolated from the Muslim community, and no Muslim would have made contact

17 *Quran 24:11*

18 *Referring to the seventh citing in the book Obscenity the Other Face of Aisha*

with him unless perforce! On the other hand, the term "Usbah" does accurately describe the group of people who attempted to defame the character of Lady Maria. These people were all closely connected to each other, as you will learn momentarily.

Additionally, as preceded in the seventh citing, the verse of Ifk reveals that two groups were reprimanded and censured for their ill action. The first was the slandering group, and the other was the one who accepted the slander and did not condemn it. The first group was addressed in the Spoken About abbreviation known as Dhameerul Ghaaib in Arabic grammar in the verses:

﴿إِنَّ الَّذينَ جاءوا بِالإِفكِ﴾

﴿لِكُلِّ امرِئٍ مِنهُم مَا اكتَسَبَ مِنَ الإِثمِ وَالَّذى تَوَلّىٰ كِبرَهُ مِنهُم لَهُ عَذابٌ عَظيمٌ﴾

﴿لَولا جاءوا عَلَيهِ بِأَربَعَةِ شُهَداءَ فَإِذ لَم يَأتوا بِالشُّهَداءِ فَأُولٰئِكَ عِندَ اللهِ هُمُ الكٰذِبونَ﴾

Indeed those who came with falsehood.

For every person among them is what [punishment] he has earned from the sin, and he who took upon himself the greater portion thereof for him is a great punishment.

Why did they [who slandered] not produce for it four witnesses? And when they do not have the witnesses, then it is they in the sight of Allah who are the liars.

However, the second group was addressed in the Spoken To abbreviation known as Dhameerul Mukhatab in the verses:

﴿لا تَحسَبوهُ شَرًّا لَكُم بَل هُوَ خَيرٌ لَكُ﴾

﴿وَلَولا فَضلُ اللَّهِ عَلَيكُم وَرَحمَتُهُ فِي الدُّنيا وَالآخِرَةِ لَمَسَّكُم في ما أَفَضتُم فيهِ عَذابٌ عَظيمٌ﴾

﴿وَلَولا إِذ سَمِعتُموهُ قُلتُم ما يَكونُ لَنا أَن نَتَكَلَّمَ بِهٰذا سُبحٰنَكَ هٰذا بُهتٰنٌ عَظيمٌ﴾

Do not think it is bad for you, instead, it is good for you.

And if it had not been for the favour of Allah upon you and His mercy in this world and the Hereafter, you would have been touched for that [lie] in which you were involved by a great punishment.

And why, when you heard it, did you not say, "It is not for us to speak of this. Exalted are You,[O Allah], this is a great slander"?.

Based on the contextual clues within the verses, it becomes apparent that the first group exerted considerable social influence, leading the second group to believe and accept the slander they spread. In contrast, the group that Aisha accused of slandering her had no known social significance or enjoyed any influential power at the time.

In brief, Lady Maria (peace be upon her) exhibited the same Quranic traits as the exonerated women in the verse of Ifk. This prompts the question of who the nefarious people responsible for slandering her were. At the same time, it raises the question of why the names of the people whom Aisha accused of slandering her are well-known, while the identities of those who slandered Lady Maria are kept anonymous in the Bakri sources.

Nonetheless, the entire story of Ifk is only described in detail in the narrations of Ahlul-Bayt (peace be upon them).[19]

---

19 *Notice what Muslim has reported in his Sahih, vol. 08, pg. 119, Anas reported that a person was charged with fornication with the slave girl of Allah's Messenger. Thereupon, Allah's Messenger said to Ali: Go and strike his neck. Ali came to him, and he found him in a well making his body cool. Ali said to him: Come out, and as he took hold of his hand and brought him out, he found that his sexual organ had been cut. Ali refrained from striking his neck. He came to Allah's Apostle and said: Allah's Messenger, he has not even the sexual organ with him.*

Al-Hakim reported in his Mustadrak, vol. 04, pg. 39, Anas reported that the mother of Ibrahim was accused of fornication with a man, so the Prophet ordered the man to be killed. However, it was later discovered that the man had been castrated.

Al-Tabarani reported in Al-Mu'jam al-Kabir, vol. 04, pg. 89, Anas reported that the Prophet's concubine, Um Ibrahim, was accused of fornication with a Coptic man, as he used to bring her water and wood to the Orchard, she was staying in. People then said, "A lout gaining access to a lout" The Prophet then ordered Ali to kill the man, but when Ali found him, he discovered that the man had been castrated as he fell from a palm tree and dropped his garment. Ali went back and told the Prophet

Reported al-Sadouq on the authority of Aamir bin Wathilah:

كنت في البيت يوم الشورى فسمعتُ علياً عليه السلام وهو يقول: استخلف النّاس أبا بكر وأنا والله أحق بالأمر وأولى به منه، واستخلف أبو بكر عمر وأنا والله أحق بالأمر وأولى به منه إلى أن قال: - إن عائشة قالت لرسول الله صلى الله عليه وآله: إن إبراهيم ليس منك وإنه ابن فلان القبطي! قال: يا علي اذهب فاقتله. فقلتُ: يا رسول الله إذا بعثتني أكونُ كالمسمار المحميّ في الوبر أو أتثبّت؟ قال: لا بل تثبّت. فذهبتُ فلمّا نظر إليَّ استند إلى حائطٍ فطرح نفسه فيه، فطرحتُ نفسي على أثره، فصعد على نخلٍ وصعدتُ خلفه، فلمّا رآني قد صعدتُ رمى بإزاره فإذا ليس له شيء مما يكون للرجال، فجئتُ فأخبرتُ رسول الله صلى الله عليه وآله فقال: الحمد لله الذي صرف عنا السوء أهل البيت.

---

what he saw. The mother of Ibrahim then gave birth to Ibrahim, but the Prophet doubted his paternity. The angel Gabriel descended and assured the Prophet that Ibrahim was his son, as he greeted Maria with: "Peace be upon you O mother of Ibrahim", the Prophet then was at peace.

The fact that the names of the people who accused Maria of adultery are deliberately concealed suggests that they are considered to be of high status in the belief of the opponents of Ahlul-Bayt and therefore protected from scrutiny.

"The day on which the caliphate council was set up - The day of consultation -, I was in the house where the gathering took place. I heard Ali (peace be upon him) say, 'The people established Abu Bakr as the Caliph while by God it was my right to oversee the affairs, and I was more deserving for that position than he was. Moreover, Abu Bakr put Umar in charge of the caliphate while by God it was my right to oversee the affairs, and I was more deserving for that position than Umar was – until he said – Aisha told Allah's Messenger, Ibrahim is not your son. He is the son of so and so the Copt. The Prophet (peace be upon him and his pure progeny) told me, 'O Ali! Go and kill him!' Then I asked God's Prophet, 'Are you sending me there as a heated iron to execute this decree as soon as I get there, or do you want me to discover the truth?' The Prophet replied, 'No. Go and discover the truth.' Then I went [as commanded], and once he saw me, he ran away into a garden. I followed him into it. Then he climbed up a date palm tree. I pursued him to the top of the tree. Once he realised that I was chasing him, he took off his undershorts, and I noticed that he had been totally castrated. Then I returned and told the Prophet about it. The Prophet (peace be upon him and his pure family) said, 'All praise is due to Allah for removing this accusation from us, the Household'.'[20]

Reported Ali ibn Ibrahim al-Qummi, on the authority of Zurarahh that he said:

---

20 *Al-Khisal by al-Sadouq, pg. 563. This Hadith is known as "Hadith al-Munashadah" in the sources of the opponents of Ahlul-Bayt such as in Musnad al-Bazar, vol. 02, pg. 237.*

سمعتُ أبا جعفر (الباقر) عليهما السلام يقول: لمّا مات إبراهيم بن رسول الله صلى الله عليه وآله حزن عليه حزناً شديداً، فقالت عائشة: ما الذي يُحزنك عليه فما هو إلاّ ابن جريح! فبعث رسول الله صلى الله عليه وآله علياً وأمره بقتله، فذهب علي عليه السلام إليه ومعه السيف، وكان جريح القبطي في حائط، وضرب علي عليه السلام باب البستان فأقبل جريح ليفتح له الباب، فلمّا رأى علياً عليه السلام عرَف في وجهه الغضب فأدبر راجعاً ولم يفتح الباب، فوثب علي عليه السلام على الحائط ونزل إلى البستان واتّبعه وولّى جريح مدبراً، فلمّا دنا منه رمى بنفسه من فوق النخلة فبدت عورته فإذا ليس له ما للرجال ولا ما للنساء، فانصرف علي عليه السلام إلى النبي صلى الله عليه وآله فقال: يا رسول الله إذا بعثتني في الأمر أكون فيه كالمسمار المحمي في الوبر أم أثبّت؟ قال، فقال: لا بل اثبتْ. فقال: والذي بعثك بالحق ما له ما للرجال ولا ما للنساء، فقال رسول الله صلى الله عليه وآله: الحمد لله الذي يصرف عنّا السوء أهل البيت.

'I heard Imam Muhammad al-Baqir (peace be upon him) say, when Ibrahim, the son of the Messenger of Allah passed away,

His Eminence was extremely aggrieved. Aisha asked, what is wrong with you? Why do you aggrieve so much on this child? Whereas it was not yours, on the contrary, it was the child of Jareeh?[21] *The Messenger of Allah summoned Ali to execute Jareeh. Ali came with the sword. Jareeh was a Copt who lived in an orchard. Ali knocked at the gate. Jareeh came behind the door to open it. When he saw Ali in fury, he ran into the orchard and did not open the gate. Ali jumped over the wall to enter the orchard and pursued him. When he realised that he was about to be killed, he climbed a tree. Ali also followed. He jumped from that tree, and as a result, his genitals were exposed, and Ali saw that he had no apparent genitals. Ali then returned to the Messenger of Allah and said, Whenever you issue an order to me, O Messenger of Allah should I act upon it immediately like a heated iron or take precaution? The Messenger of Allah replied, No, you should exercise precaution. Ali said, by Allah, who sent you with truth, Jareeh is neither a male nor a female. The Messenger of Allah said, All praise is due to Allah, Who removed this evil from us, the Ahlul-Bayt".*[22]

Reported al-Hussain ibn Hamdan al-Khusaibi and Muhammad ibn Jareer al-Tabari on the authority of Muhammad ibn Ismail al-Hassani, from Abu Muhammad al-Hassan al-Askari (peace be upon him), said:

---

21 *It may be pronounced Juraih*

22 *Tafsir al-Qummi, vol. 02, pg. 99*

هل علمتم ما قد رُميت به مارية القبطية ما ادُّعيَ عليها في ولادتها إبراهيم بن رسول الله؟ قالوا: لا يا سيدنا أنت أعلم، فخبِّرنا لنعلم. قال: إنَّ مارية لمّا أُهديَتْ إلى جدي رسول الله صلى الله عليه وآله أُهديت مع جَوارٍ قسَّمهنّ رسول الله على أصحابه، وظنَّ بمارية من دونهنّ، وكان معها خادم يقال له جريح يؤدبها بآداب الملوك، وأسلمت على يد رسول الله صلى الله عليه وآله وأسلم جريح معها، وحسن إيمانهما وإسلامهما، فملكت مارية قلب رسول الله صلى الله عليه وآله، فحسدها بعض أزواج رسول الله صلى الله عليه وآله، وأقبلت عائشة وحفصة تشكوان إلى أبويهما ميل رسول الله صلى الله عليه وآله إلى مارية وإيثاره إياها عليهما، حتى سوّلت لأبويهما أنفسهما أن يقولا: إن مارية إنما حملت بإبراهيم من جريح! وكانوا لا يظنون جريحاً خادماً زمنا. فأقبل أبواهما إلى رسول الله صلى الله عليه وآله وهو جالس في مسجده، فجلسا بين يديه، وقالا: يا رسول الله ما يحِلُّ لنا ولا يسعنا أن نكتمك ما ظهرنا عليه من خيانة واقعة بك. قال: وماذا تقولان!؟ قالا: يا رسول الله إن جريحاً يأتي من مارية الفاحشة العظمى! وإن حملها من جريح وليس هو منك يا رسول الله! فأربدَ وجه رسول

الله صلى الله عليه وآله وتلَّونَ لِعِظَمِ ما تلقَّياهُ به، ثم قال: ويحكما ما تقولان!؟ فقالا: يا رسول الله إننا خلّفنا جريحاً ومارية في مشربة وهو يفاكهها ويلاعبها ويروم منها ما تروم الرجال من النساء! فابعث إلى جريح فإنك تجده على هذه الحال، فأنفذْ فيه حكمك وحكم الله تعالى. فقال النبي صلى الله عليه وآله: يا أبا الحسن خذ معك سيفك ذا الفقار، حتى تمضي إلى مشربة مارية، فإن صادفتها وجريحا كما يصفان فاخمدهما ضربا. فقام علي واتشح بسيفه وأخذه تحت ثوبه، فلّما ولّى ومرَّ من بين يدي رسول الله أتى إليه راجعا، فقال له: يا رسول الله أكونُ فيما أمرتني كالسكّة المُحماةِ في النار أو الشاهد يرى ما لا يرى الغائب؟ فقال النبي صلى الله عليه وآله: فديتك يا علي، بل الشاهد يرى ما لا يرى الغائب. قال: فأقبل علي عليه السلام وسيفة في يده حتى تسوّر من فوق مشربة مارية، وهي جالسة وجريح معها، يؤدّبها بآداب الملوك، ويقول لها: أعظمي رسول الله وكنّيه وأكرميه. ونحو من هذا الكلام. حتى نظر جريح إلى أمير المؤمنين وسيفه مُشْهَرٌ بيده، ففزع منه جريح، وأتى إلى نخلة في دار المشربة فصعد إلى رأسها، فنزل أمير المؤمنين إلى المشربة، وكشف الريح عن أثواب جريح، فانكشف

ممسوحا. فقال: انزل يا جريج. فقال: يا أمير المؤمنين آمن على نفسي؟ قال: آمن على نفسك. قال: فنزل جريح، وأخذ بيده أمير المؤمنين، وجاء به إلى رسول الله صلى الله عليه وآله، فأوقفه بين يديه، وقال له: يا رسول الله، إن جريحاً خادم ممسوح. فولّى النبي بوجهه إلى الجدار، وقال: حُلَّ لهما لعنهما الله يا جريح واكشف عن نفسك حتى يتبين كذبهما، ويحهما ما أجرأهما على الله وعلى رسوله! فكشف جريح أثوابه فإذا هو خادم ممسوح كما وصف. فسقطا بين يدي رسول الله وقالا: يا رسول الله التوبة! استغفر لنا فلن نعود! فقال رسول الله صلى الله عليه وآله: لا تاب الله عليكما! فما ينفعكما استغفاري ومعكما هذه الجرأة على الله وعلى رسوله!؟ قالا: يا رسول الله فإن استغفرت لنا رجوْنا أن يغفر لنا ربنا! فأنزل الله الآية بهما وفي براءة مارية: ﴿إِنَّ الَّذينَ يَرمونَ المُحصَنٰتِ الغٰفِلٰتِ المُؤمِنٰتِ لُعِنوا فِي الدُّنيا وَالءاخِرَةِ وَلَهُم عَذابٌ عَظيمٌ﴾ ﴿يَومَ تَشهَدُ عَلَيهِم أَلسِنَتُهُم وَأَيديهِم وَأَرجُلُهُم بِما كانوا يَعمَلونَ﴾

"Abul Hassan al-Rida (peace be upon him) said to the ones who were in his presence from his Shia: 'Do you know what Maria the Copt was slandered with, and what was alleged upon her regarding her new-born Ibrahim, the son of the Messenger

of Allah?' They said: 'O our Master, you certainly are more knowing, therefore inform us!'

"So, he said: 'When Maria was gifted to my grandfather, the Messenger of Allah (peace be upon him and his family), she was accompanied with other concubines, who were given out, so he attained her[23] *from beside his companions. And there was a eunuch servant with her called Jareeh, and both committed to the faith. Then Maria attracted the heart of the Messenger of Allah (peace be upon him and his family), and some of his wives envied her. So, Aisha and Hafsa came to their fathers complaining about the inclination of the Messenger of Allah towards Maria and preference of her over them, unto the extent that it induced them and their fathers themselves they slander Maria that she is pregnant with Ibrahim, from Jareeh, and they - Abu Bakr and Umar - were not thinking that Jareeh is a servant.*

"So, their fathers came to the Messenger of Allah, and he was seated in his mosque, and they both sat down in front of him, then said, 'O Messenger of Allah! It is not permissible for us, nor do we have any leeway that we should conceal upon you what has appeared from the occurrence of betrayal with you. He (peace be upon him and his progeny) said: 'What is that you two are saying?' They said, 'O Messenger of Allah! Jareeh came to Maria with grievous immorality, and she is pregnant from him, and it isn't from you!'

---

23 He (peace be upon him and his pure progeny) chose her to become the mother of his child.

"So, the face of the Messenger of Allah reddened and paled (out of wrath), and there was displayed to him the obscenity of the grievousness of what they were facing him with. Then he said: 'Woe be unto you two! What are you saying?' They said, 'O Messenger of Allah! We left behind Jareeh and Maria in her chamber, and he was patting her and playing with her, and he wished from her what the man wished from the woman. Therefore send [someone] to Jareeh, and you will find him upon this state, and implement with regards to him, the Judgment of Allah!'

"So, the Prophet bent over towards Ali, then said: 'O Abu Al Hassan! Arise, O my brother, and with you is Dhul Fiqar - the sword - until you go to the orchard of Maria. So, if these two are truthful and Jareeh is as they are describing him to be, then put them both down with a strike of your sword'. So, Ali arose and took his sword and placed it beneath his clothes. But, when he turned from in front of the Messenger of Allah, he bent down to him and said: 'O Messenger of Allah, I will be, regarding what you instructed me for, like the knife shielded in the wool, or the one present would see what the absentees did not?' So, the Prophet said, May I be your sacrifice, O Ali! But the one present will see what the absentees did not.

"So, Ali went, and his sword was in his hand until he surveyed from above the orchard of Maria, and she was seated inside of the chamber, and Jareeh was with her, assisting her with the etiquettes of the slaves, and he was saying to her, revere the Messenger of Allah, and listen to him, and honour him, and approximately this speech, until Jareeh turned towards the

commander of the faithful, and his bare sword was in his hand. So, Jareeh panicked to a palm tree in the orchard and climbed up to its top. The commander of the faithful came down to the orchard, and the wind uncovered the clothes of Jareeh, and he was a eunuch servant. So, he said to him, descend, O Jareeh! He said, O commander of the faithful! Is there safety upon myself? He said: There is safety upon yourself.

"Jareeh descended, and the commander of the faithful grabbed his hand and came with him to the Messenger of Allah, and paused him in front of him, and said to him: 'O Messenger of Allah! Jareeh is a eunuch servant!' So, the Messenger of Allah turned his face towards the wall, and he said, there is a release for yourself, may Allah curse them both, O Jareeh, to the extent that their lying is exposed and their disgrace and their crime against Allah and against his Messenger. Both - Abu Bakr and Umar - fell in front of the Messenger of Allah and said, O Messenger of Allah! The repentance. Seek Forgiveness for us! The Messenger said, there is no turning of Allah [with mercy] upon you two; therefore, my seeking forgiveness would not benefit you, and with you is this audacity.

"Then Allah Revealed regarding both [Abu Bakr and Umar]: {Surely those who accuse chaste married women, the unaware believing women, would be cursed in this world and the Hereafter, and for them is a grievous Punishment. On the Day, their tongues will testify against them, and their hands, and their legs, with what they had been doing]".[24]

---

24 *Al-Hidayah al-Kubra by al-Khusaibi, pg. 297, Dala'il al-Imamah by al-Tabari al-Imami, pg. 385, Tafsir al-Burhan by al-Bahrani, vol. 03, pg. 129*

According to Shia Muslim literature, it is a firmly held belief that the Quranic verses of Ifk were revealed with the explicit purpose of clearing Maria of an accusation levelled against her by Aisha. This is what has reached us from the Imams of Ahlul-Bayt (peace be upon them), a matter confirmed by Ali ibn Ibrahim al-Qummi in his well-known Quran exegesis book as he states:

وأما قوله: ﴿إِنَّ الَّذِينَ جاءوا بِالإِفْكِ عُصبَةٌ مِنكُم لا تَحسَبوهُ شَرًّا لَكُم بَل هُوَ خَيرٌ لَكُم﴾

فإن العامة رووا أنها نزلت في عائشة وما رُميت به في غزوة بني المصطلق من خزاعة، وأما الخاصة فإنهم رووا أنها نزلت في مارية القبطية وما رمتها به عائشة.

"As for the verse: {Indeed, those who came with falsehood are a group among you}. Do not think it is bad for you; rather it is good for you., the opponents of Ahlul-Bayt narrate this verse about Aisha when during the Battle of Bani Mustaliq, she was accused of relations with a man from the Khuza'a tribe, but the followers of Ahlul-Bayt narrate that it was revealed about Maria the Copt, against whom Aisha made allegations of unfaithfulness".[25]

These fragments of history brought four individuals to light; Abu Bakr and Umar, along with their daughters Aisha

25 *Tafsir al-Qummi, vol. 02, pg. 99*

and Hafsa, conspired together to frame the mother of Ibrahim (peace be upon them both) for adultery. This fact is consistent with the Quranic expression, which precisely described them as {Usbah., a group of people conspired to cunningly concoct to accomplish their malicious plan. This finding has also been noted by prominent Shia clerics, such as the late Sayed Muhammad al-Shirazi, known as al-Mujadid al-Thani[26], the second reformer, who states in his Quran exegesis that the reason behind the use of such specific Quranic phrase is to signify that the quad deliberately acted out of malice, to achieve their shared ill aim.[27]

ولعلّ الإتيان بهذه الخصوصية لإفادة أن الإفك إنما كان وليد جماعة ذات هدف واحد، فليس كلاماً قاله مغرض، وإنما حركة مقصودة ضد الرسول صلى الله عليه وآله.

The quad's apparent connection to the Prophet (peace be upon him and his pure progeny) gave them a platform in the society through which their words were heeded by others. Therefore, the verses of Ifk were revealed to refute the quad's lies and slander. As a result, the verses are closer to the events concerning Lady Maria (peace be upon her) than any other account.

---

26 *Also known as Imam al-Shirazi and the Sultan of authors.*

27 *Taqrib al-Adhan, by Imam al-Shirazi may Allah elevate his ranks, vol. 03, pg. 685*

THE RINGLEADER OF THE SLANDER

However, it could also be argued that if Aisha was the ringleader of the slander, then why does the verse "and he who took upon himself the greater portion thereof – for him is a great punishment"[28] refer to the one who took the greatest part in the slander using masculine pronouns. This may suggest that the one who was most responsible for the slander was a man.

The answer to this question is: It is linguistically allowed to use a masculine pronoun for a feminine noun and vice versa, as this is a customary practice amongst Arabs based on what is known as Haml al Lafdh ala al Ma'na. This means that if a word is morphemically feminine, it might be put in a masculine context if the meaning of the word is semantically masculine and vice versa. This has been noted by linguistic and grammarian al-Tha'alibi[29] in Fiqh al-Lugha.

---

28 Quran 24:11

29 Fiqh al-Tha'alibi, Chapter 25, pg. 365

The Holy Quran contains ample examples of this:

﴿فإن يكن منكم مائة صابرة يغلبوا مائتين﴾

So, if there are a hundred (feminine) steadfast among you, they will overcome (masculine) two hundred.[30]

Although it is morphemically feminine, the word مائة is put in a masculine context, followed by the verb يغلبوا . This is to metaphorically carry out the reference to the forbearing male fighters concerned in the verse.

﴿ولا يقبل منها شفعة﴾

No intercession (feminine) will be accepted (masculine)[31]

In this verse, the word شفعة is put in a masculine context, although it ends in ta-marbuta, which is a feminine morpheme because the meaning was metaphorically carried out to the request of asking for intercession, known as طلب الشفاعة

Similarly, in the verse:

﴿فيومئذ لا ينفع الذين ظلموا معذرتهم﴾

---

30 Quran 8:66

31 Quran 2:48

The wrongdoers' excesses (feminine) will not benefit them (masculine)[32]

The word يَنفَعُ is used, although it is masculine, for مَعذِرَتُهُم , which is feminine. This is because the verse is pointing towards the meaning of the action of requesting to be excused الاستعذار.

The same concept applies in the following verses:

﴿وَما يُدريكَ لَعَلَّ السّاعَةَ قَريبٌ﴾

You never know, perhaps the Hour (السّاعَةَ feminine) is near (قَريبٌ masculine)[33]

In contrast to the wording Lafdh, the word السّاعَةَ is put in a masculine context, although it is feminine to carry out the meaning of Time metaphorically.

﴿بَل كَذَّبوا بِالسّاعَةِ وَأَعتَدنا لِمَن كَذَّبَ بِالسّاعَةِ سَعيرًا﴾

﴿إِذا رَأَتهُم مِن مَكانٍ بَعيدٍ سَمِعوا لَها تَغَيُّظًا وَزَفيرًا﴾

In fact, they deny the Hour. And for the deniers of the Hour, we have prepared a blazing Fire (سَعيرًا masculine).

---

32 *Quran 30:57*

33 *Quran 42:17*

Once it sees them from a distance, they will hear her (لَهَا feminine) fuming and growling.[34]

Again, in contrast to the wording Lafdh, the word سَعِيرًا is put in a feminine context, although it is masculine to carry out the meaning of Fire metaphorically.

In addition, there are words in the Quran which come in both masculine and feminine forms. One example of many is the word لطَّٰغُوتِ in Surat An-Nisa:

أَلَم تَرَ إِلَى الَّذينَ يَزعُمونَ أَنَّهُم ءامَنوا بِما أُنزِلَ إِلَيكَ وَما أُنزِلَ مِن قَبلِكَ يُريدونَ أَن يَتَحاكَموا إِلَى ﴿الطّٰغوتِ وَقَد أُمِروا أَن يَكفُروا بِهِ﴾

Have you "O Prophet" not seen those who claim they believe in what has been revealed to you and what was revealed before you? They seek the judgment of false judges. [35]

The word الطَّٰغُوتِ came in the masculine form as it was followed by بِهِ whereas in Surat Az-Zumar:

﴿وَالَّذينَ اجتَنَبُوا الطّٰغوتَ أَن يَعبُدوها وَأَنابوا إِلَى اللَّهِ لَهُمُ البُشرىٰ فَبَشِّر عِبادِ﴾

---

34 Quran 25:11-12

35 Quran 04:60

And those who shun the worship of false gods, turning to Allah "alone", will have good news.[36]

The word الطّٰغوتَ was feminine as it was followed by يَعبُدوها. Similarly, although Aisha was meant in the verse:

﴿وَالَّذى تَوَلّىٰ كِبرَهُ مِنهُم لَهُ عَذابٌ عَظيمٌ﴾

And he who took upon himself the greater portion thereof – for him is a great punishment.[37]

We find it tagged as masculine. This is because the rule of Haml al Lafdh ala al Ma'na applies where كِبرَهُ is masculine, referring to the meaning of masterminding the slander and persisting in spreading the untruth known as

معنى أكبر العصبة في الإفك والافتراء

Correspondingly, the same rule applies in the verse:

﴿يٰأَيُّهَا الَّذينَ ءامَنوا إِن جاءَكُم فاسِقٌ بِنَبَإٍ﴾

"If an evildoer brings you any news"[38] referring to Aisha when she vilified Lady Maria (peace be upon her).

Commented Ali ibn Ibrahim al-Qummi in his Tafsir:

---

36 Quran 39:17

37 Quran 24:11

38 Quran 49:06

وقوله: يٰأَيُّهَا الَّذينَ ءامَنوا إِن جاءَكُم فاسِقٌ بِنَبَإٍ فَتَبَيَّنوا أَن تُصيبوا قَومًا بِجَهٰلَةٍ فَتُصبِحوا عَلىٰ ما فَعَلتُم نٰدِمينَ فإنها نزلت في مارية القبطية أم إبراهيم عليه السلام، وكان سبب ذلك أن عائشة قالت لرسول الله صلى الله عليه وآله: إن إبراهيم ليس هو منك وإنما هو من جريح القبطي إنه يدخل إليها في كل يوم! فغضب رسول الله صلى الله عليه وآله وقال لأمير المؤمنين عليه السلام: خذ السيف وائتني برأس جريح، فأخذ أمير المؤمنين عليه السلام السيف ثم قال: بأبي أنت وأمي يا رسول الله، إنك إذا بعثتني في أمر أكون فيه كالسفود المحماة في الوبر فكيف تأمرني؟ أثبَّتُ فيه أو أمضِ على ذلك؟ فقال له رسول الله صلى الله عليه وآله: بل تثبَّتْ. فجاء أمير المؤمنين عليه السلام إلى مشربة إم إبراهيم فتسلّق عليها، فلما نظر إليه جريح هرب منه وصعد النخلة، فدنا منه أمير المؤمنين عليه السلام وقال له: انزل! فقال له: يا علي اتّق الله ما هاهنا أناس (ما هاهنا بأس) إني مجبوب! ثم كشف عن عورته فإذا هو مجبوب. فأتى به إلى رسول الله صلى الله عليه وآله فقال له رسول الله صلى الله عليه وآله: ما شأنك يا جريح؟ فقال: يا رسول الله إن القبط يجبّون حشمهم ومن يدخل إلى أهليهم،

والقبطيون لا يأنسون إلا بالقبطيين، فبعثني أبوها لأدخل إليها وأخدمها وأؤنسها. فأنزل الله عزّ وجل: يٰأَيُّهَا الَّذينَ ءامَنوا إِن جاءَكُم فاسِقٌ بِنَبَإٍ.. الآية.

"As for the verse: {O believers, if an evildoer brings you any news, verify "it" so you do not harm people unknowingly, becoming regretful for what you have done.}, it has been revealed about Maria the Copt, the mother of Ibrahim (peace be upon him). Aisha made an accusation against her when she remarked to the Messenger of Allah (peace be upon him and his pure family): Ibrahim was not your son, he was a son of Jareeh's the Copt, for he gains access to where she [Maria] is every single day. The Messenger of Allah (peace be upon him and his pure family) became infuriated and summoned the commander of the faithful (peace be upon him) and told him to cut off the head of Jareeh. The commander of the faithful posthaste wielded the sword and remarked heedfully: 'May my parents be sacrificed for you, O Messenger of Allah; you are sending me on a duty; I shall perform it immediately like a heated rod[39] enters the camel fur, or I shall hold my ground and wait until the truth is known to me? The Messenger of Allah (peace be upon him and his pure progeny) said: 'You shall hold your ground and not make haste in this matter'. The commander of the faithful then came to the orchard of the mother of Ibrahim. When Jareeh saw the commander of the faithful scale the wall of the orchard, Jareeh fled from there and

39 Meaning to obsequiously to execute the command immediately without delay.

climbed a date tree. The commander of the faithful followed in pursuit. When he drew closer and commanded him: 'Come down'! Jareeh said: 'O Ali, fear Allah, for there are no people here,[40] I am completely castrated!' He uncovered himself, and he was truly as he described. So, the commander of the faithful then brought him to the Messenger of Allah (peace be upon him and his pure progeny), who asked what the matter was, O Jareeh. He explained, O Messenger of Allah, it is a customary practice among the Copts that the servants who go into their houses are made castrated, and Maria's father sent me as her servant to serve and attend to her needs. The Prophet said: "All praise is due to Allah, Who keeps away all evils from us and Who exposes the lies of the liars. The verse {O believers, if an evildoer brings you any news, verify "it" so you do not harm people unknowingly, becoming regretful for what you have done.} was hence revealed".[41]

40 *Or he might have said: "for there is no problem".*

41 *Tafsir al-Qummi, vol. 02, pg. 319, the narration should not be dismissed due to minor differences, such as the fact that Jareeh exposed himself or that Maria's father sent him to serve her. This narration is transmitted by meaning and rephrased by Ali ibn Ibrahim.*

MANIFEST AND LATENT MEANINGS

Some people may argue that the verse was revealed in reference to the hypocrite al-Walid ibn Uqba. How can we reconcile this argument with the claim that it was revealed to condemn Aisha's accusation against Lady Maria?

The answer to this conundrum is that it is gathered from the narrations and traditions that the Quran descended on the night of Qadr and then gradually in portions after that. Some of the verses repeatedly came down on different occasions. This is to emphasise the significance of the events concerning the verses, and thus the repetition results in etching the meaning of the verses to the minds. It is also gathered that some verses have more than one interpretation. This is known as the recognition of Tafsir and Taweel and al-Ma'na al-Dhahir (i.e., exterior or apparent meaning) and al-Batin (i.e., latent or hidden meaning). This verse is commensurate with the same rule explained.

In a recount of the accusation of Ifk against Lady Maria, it has been narrated that Imam Abu Jaffar al-Baqir (peace be upon him) said:

فتهلّل وجه رسول الله صلى الله عليه وآله وقال: الحمد لله الذي لم يزل يعافينا أهل البيت من سوء ما يلطّخونا. فأنزل الله عز وجل: يٰأَيُّهَا الَّذينَ ءامَنوا إِن جاءَكُم فاسِقٌ بِنَبَإٍ. الآية. فقال زرارة لأبي جعفر عليه السلام: إن العامة يقولون: نزلت هذه الآية في الوليد بن عقبة بن أبي معيط حين جاء إلى النبي صلى الله عليه وآله فأخبره عن بني خزيمة أنهم كفروا حين جاء إلى النبي صلى الله عليه وآله فأخبره عن بني خزيمة أنهم كفروا بعد إسلامهم؟ فقال عليه السلام: يا زرارة، أَوَ ما علمتَ أنه ليس من القرآن آية إلاّ ولها ظهر وبطن؟ فهذا الذي في أيدي الناس ظهرها، والذي حدّثتك به بطنها. ولمّا نهاهم الله سبحانه عن اتّباع قول الفاسق وأمرهم بالتثبّت في الأمر نبّههم على أن فيهم رسول الله صلى الله عليه وآله وأن أخبار الأرض والسماء عنده، فخذوا عنه ودعوا قول الفاسق.

"The face of the Messenger of Allah (peace be upon him and his pure progeny) beamed with joy thereof and said: 'May all praise be to Allah, Who continues to drive away smear from us

the Ahlul-Bayt'. Allah The Most Exalted therefore revealed: {O believers, if an evildoer brings you any news, verify "it" so you do not harm people unknowingly, becoming regretful for what you have done.}. So Zurarah asked Abu Jaffar (peace be upon him): your opponents claim that it has been revealed about al-Walid ibn Uqbah ibn Abu Mu'eet when he once informed the Prophet (peace be upon him and his pure progeny) about Banu Khuzaima renouncing Islam? The Imam (peace be upon him) said: 'O Zurarah, did you not know that each verse of the Quran has manifest and latent meanings? What people know is only its apparent meaning, and I have informed you about its hidden meaning'".[42]

---

42 *Ta'weel al-Ayat by Sharaf ad-Deen al-Hussaini an-Najafi, vol. 02, pg. 604*

ANSWERING THE DILEMMAS

However, there remain two questions that defy resolution: First, how did the Prophet (peace be upon him and his pure progeny) order the killing of the servant based on the quad's accusation without the testimony of four righteous witnesses or a confession from the adulterer himself? How did he order the killing in the first place when the ruling in such a case, assuming it has been proven, would be lashing or stoning in the crime of adultery?

Imam al-Sadiq (peace be upon him) unravelled this mystery as he explained that the Holy Prophet (peace be upon him and his pure progeny) did not intend to kill the servant but rather was seeking to prove his innocence to the public and to show Aisha, the main accuser, the error of her ways and to realise that she was about to kill an innocent man. But alas! Aisha was neither remorseful nor repentant.

Reported Ali ibn Ibrahim al-Qummi, Abdullah ibn Bukair narrated:

قلتُ لأبي عبد الله عليه السلام: جُعلت فداك، كان رسول الله صلى الله عليه وآله أمر بقتل القبطي وقد عَلِمَ أنها قد كذبت عليه أو لم يعلم وإنما دفع الله عن القبطي بتثبّت علي عليه السلام؟ فقال: بلى قد كان والله أعلم، ولو كانت عزيمة من رسول الله صلى الله عليه وآله القتل ما رجع علي عليه السلام حتى يقتله، ولكن إنما فعل رسول الله صلى الله عليه وآله لترجع عن ذنبها، فما رجعتْ ولا اشتدّ عليها قتل رجل مسلم بكذبها!

"I asked Abu Abdullah al-Sadiq (peace be upon him): May I be sacrificed for you, did the Messenger of Allah (peace be upon him and his pure progeny) order the killing of the Coptic servant? Did he know that she had lied, or did he not know? Did Allah drive away the killing of the Coptic because Ali verified the matter? He said: 'Indeed, the Messenger was more aware that it was an allegation, but he commanded thus due to exigency. Had the Messenger of Allah (peace be upon him and his pure progeny) ordered the killing truly and seriously, Ali would not have returned without putting the Messenger's command into effect. However, he only commanded it so that when Aisha came to know that an innocent person was being

killed because of her lie, she would repent from her sins. But alas! She neither repented nor felt remorseful for wanting to kill an innocent man".[43]

This response aligns with Ibn Hazm's perspective, who is an opponent. He asserted that the Prophet (peace be upon him and his pure progeny) did not intend to kill the servant but aimed to prove his innocence and reveal the falsehoods against him. Ibn Hazm stated:

ومعاذ الله أن يأمر رسول الله صلى الله عليه وسلم بقتل أحدٍ بظنٍّ بغير إقرار إو بيّنة أو علم مشاهدة أو وحي، أو أن يأمر بقتله دونها، لكن رسول الله صلى الله عليه وسلم قد علم يقينا أنه بريء وأن القول كذب، فأراد عليه السلام أن يوقِفَ على ذلك مشاهدة، فأمر بقتله لو فعل ذلك الذي قيل عنه، فكان هذا حكماً صحيحاً فيمن آذى رسول الله صلى الله عليه وسلم، وقد عليم عليه السلام أن القتل لا ينفذ عليه لما يظهر الله تعالى من براءته.

"God forbid, the Messenger of Allah (peace be upon him) ever orders the killing of someone based on assumptions, or without confession, witnesses, evident proof, or divine revelation. The Messenger of Allah (peace be upon him) was undoubtedly

43 *Tafsir al-Qummi, vol. 02, pg. 319, Bihar al-Anwar by al-Alama al-Majlisi, vol. 22, pg. 154*

aware of his innocence and that the accusations against him were false. He, therefore, wanted to verify this by the sighting. He would only order the killing [of the servant] if he had clear and convincing evidence that he committed what he had been accused of. This was a proper judgement for whoever intended to harm the Messenger of Allah (peace be upon him). He (peace be upon him) knew [through divine knowledge] that [the servant] would be saved from the killing because Allah The Most Exalted would reveal his innocence.'[44]

Second, how did the Prophet (peace be upon him and his pure family) not apply the penalty of slander, Hadd al-Qadhf, on Aisha and her group after it had been proven that they maliciously intended to frame Lady Maria (peace be upon her)?

The answer to this question is: According to belief, the Prophet (peace be upon him and his progeny) holds the highest level of authority. This means that he has the power to suspend or prevent punishment for the greater good. A prime example is when Khalid Ibn al-Walid deserved punishment for his actions towards Banu Jadhimah,[45] but the Prophet (peace be upon him and his progeny) chose not to apply it. Similarly, when

---

44 Al-Muhala by ibn Hazm, vol. 11, pg. 414, we of course do not deem everything in the narration correct

45 A well-known incident where the Prophet (peace be upon him and his pure progeny) said: "By Allah! I disassociate myself from what Khalid ibn al-Walid has done" and repeated it twice. Sahih Bukhari, Book 93, Hadith 51.

individuals attempted to assassinate him at Aqabah,[46] he (peace be upon him and his progeny) did not administer punishment. Imam al-Baqir (peace be upon him) revealed that Aisha will not escape punishment; it has only been adjourned until the reappearance of the 12th Imam al-Mahdi (peace be upon him and may Allah hasten his reappearance) when Aisha will be brought back and lashed.[47]

Narrated al-Barqi and al-Saduq, on the authority of Abdul-Rahman al-Qasir:

قال لي أبو جعفر عليه السلام: أمّا لو قد قام قائمنا عليه السلام لقد رُدَّت إليه الحميراء حتى يجلدها الحدّ وحتى ينتقم لابنة محمد صلى الله عليه وآله فاطمة عليها السلام منها. قلتُ: جُعلت فداك، ولمَ يجلدها الحدّ؟ قال: لفريتها على أم إبراهيم عليهما السلام. قلتُ: فكيف آخَّرَه الله للقائم؟ فقال: لأن الله تبارك وتعالى بعث محمداً

46 *More details of the incident of Aqaba is found in Sheikh al-Habib's book Obscenity the other face of Aisha pg. 165. When it was said to the Prophet (peace be upon him and his pure progeny): "O Messenger of Allah why do you not order them to be killed? He said: I would detest that people may say that Muhammad kills his companions". Al-Sira an-Nabawiya by Ibn Kathir, vol. 04, pg. 34.*

47 *Sheikh al-Habib: "I have asked Allah The Most Exalted to grant me the privilege to perform this myself before my master Sahib al-Zaman (peace be upon him) and I do humbly request my fellow believing brethren to pray for this to happen".*

صلى الله عليه وآله رحمة، وبعث القائم عليه السلام نقمة.

"Abu Jaffar al-Baqir (peace be upon him) told me, When the Qaim rises, Humaira will be brought to him (after being raised from the dead), so that he may punish her with lashes avenge for Fatima, the daughter of Muhammad (peace be upon him and his pure progeny). I then asked, may I be sacrificed for you, why he would punish her with lashes? He replied, due to the false allegation she made against Ibrahim's mother. I asked how is that the Almighty Allah postponed this matter of punishment till the time of Qaim's reappearance; he said, The Almighty Allah sent Muhammad (peace be upon him and his pure progeny) as mercy, but He has sent the Qa'im for punishing and taking revenge".[48]

48 *Al-Mahasin by Ahmed Ibn Muhammad Ibn Khalid al-Barqi, vol. 02, pg. 239, Ilal al-Sharai' by as-Sadouq, vol. 02, pg. 580. What he means by "He has sent the Qa'im for punishing and taking revenge", is that he will take revenge from tyrants and disbelievers according to Islamic law. This was not a divine duty assigned to the Holy Prophet (peace be upon him and his pure progeny) in many cases for the importance of establishing conformity, as it was fundamentally pivotal to strengthening the religion in its early stages and avoiding internal strife. This is the reason why he wisely avoided killing those so-called companions who plotted to assassinate him at Aqabah and strategically avoided killing the hypocrites such as Abdullah ibn Ubay ibn Saloul as it was mentioned in Sahih Bukhari: "So, that people may not say that Muhammad kills his companions". This was in accordance with Allah's clear command to the Prophet: "Only Allah knows what is in their hearts. So, turn away from them, caution them, and give them advice that will shake their very souls." Quran 04:63*

Abu Bakr and Umar will also be brought back and declared criminals at the time of the Qa'im (peace be upon him). The Hirabah Hadd[49] will be applied, and they will be crucified for their crimes, which includes accusing Lady Maria (peace be upon her). The Hadiths are replete with accounts of this incident taking place. One example is a long narration by al-Hussain ibn Hamdan al-Khusaibi: On the authority of al-Mufadhal ibn Umar, Imam Jaffar al-Sadiq (peace be upon him) said:

ثم يأمر بإنزالهما فيُنزلا إليه فيحييهما بإذن الله تعالى ويأمر الخلائق بالاجتماع، ثم يقصّ عليهم قصص فعالهما في كل كوّْر ودور (...) كل ذلك يعدّده عليه السلام عليهما، ويلزمهما إياه فيعترفان به ثم يأمر بهما فيقتص منهما في ذلك الوقت بمظالم من حضر، ثم يصلبهما على الشجرة ويأمر نارا تخرج من الأرض فتحرقهما والشجرة ثم يأمر ريحاً فتنسفهما في اليَمِّ نسفاً. قال المفضّل: يا سيدي ذلك آخر عذابهما؟ قال: هيهات يا مفضّل! والله لَيرِدَنَّ وليحضُرَنَّ السيّد الأكبر محمد رسول الله صلى الله عليه وآله والصدّيق الأكبر أمير المؤمنين وفاطمة والحسن والحسين والأئمة عليهم

49 *Hadd al-Hirabah is mentioned in the verse: {Indeed, the penalty for those who wage war against Allah and His Messenger and spread mischief in the land is death, crucifixion, cutting off their hands and feet on opposite sides, or exile from the land. This "penalty" is a disgrace for them in this world, and they will suffer a tremendous punishment in the Hereafter} Quran 05:33*

السلام وكل من محض الإيمان محضاً أو محض الكفر محضاً، وليقتَصَّنَّ منهما لجميعهم حتى أنهما ليُقْتَلان في كل يوم وليلة ألف قتلة! ويُرَدّان إلى ما شاء ربهما.

"So, they will be brought down to him, and he will bring them back to life with the permission of Allah the Most High, and he will order all creatures to gather together. Then, he will narrate to them stories of what both did during every age and epoch (…) he will charge all of that against them both, and will accuse them of everything, and they both will confess to everything. He would make the two of them responsible for all of them, and they would also confess to being responsible for them. Then he would announce that whoever has suffered any injustice at their hand should take retaliation from them, and they will do that. Then he would have them hanged from the tree again and then issue a command by which a fire would emerge from the ground and burn them along with the tree on which they are impaled. After that, he would order the wind to blow their ashes to the seas."

"Al-Mufadhal asked: Master, is it the last chastisement they would suffer? The Imam replied: How far! O al-Mufadhal, by Allah, they shall be brought back again at a time when the Holy Prophet, the truthful commander of the faithful, Lady Fatima, Imam Hasan, Imam Husayn and the Holy Imams (peace be upon them). Every sincere believer and every complete disbeliever will be present. All shall take retaliation from those two, so much so that they shall be killed a thousand times

every day and every night. Every time they are revived by the command of Allah, they shall be punished again".[50]

Based on the promise made by the Imam (peace be upon him) regarding the resurrection of all complete non-believers, Hafsa will also be brought back. This means that everyone involved in the accusation made against Lady Maria will be retaliated against during that time.

---

50 Al-Hidaya al-Kubra by al-Khusaiby, pg. 400, Mukhtasar Basa'ir ad-Darajat by al-Sheikh Hassan Ibn Sulaiman al-Hilli, pg. 189, Bihar al-Anwar by al-Alama al-Majlisi, vol. 53, pg. 12.

THE IFK IS SOLVED

Upon conducting extensive research and meticulous analysis, a definitive truth has been uncovered regarding the story of Ifk. The evidence gleaned from the traditions of the pure household (peace be upon them) is in complete alignment with the Holy Book, logical reasoning, and historical records. This, in turn, directly contradicts the fictitious narrative propagated by Aisha.

In conclusion, this research has provided a new perspective on the Ifk incident, and it has shown that the truth may not be what it is claimed to be. The research has shown that the traditions of the Ahlul-Bayt (peace be upon them) are supported by the traditions found in the sources of their opponents, which were narrated by Aisha herself. The research has also shown that the names of the accusers of Lady Maria (peace be upon her) have been concealed in the sources of the opponents of Ahlul-Bayt, which suggests that they are held in high esteem and considered beyond reproach. This is not surprising, considering that the opponents of Ahlul-Bayt had previously hidden the identities of those who plotted to assassinate the Prophet (peace be upon him and his pure progeny) at Aqaba when they pelted the convoy with rocks, attempting to have it slipped and fallen off the mountain and eventually kill the Prophet.

Furthermore, the research has shown that it is Abu Bakr, Umar, Aisha, and Hafsa, who were involved in the Ifk incident and that their names have been concealed to protect their reputations. This is supported by Aisha's own statement, where she deliberately feigned any similarity between the Prophet and his son Ibrahim, citing her overwhelming jealousy as the reason. This suggests that she was willing to support the slanderer's claim against the Prophet purely to feed her jealousy.

The research has also shown that Aisha was able to twist the truth to her advantage when she gained consolidated power later. She used her power to promote her own mythical fabricated hadiths at a time when there was no one to challenge her authority or stand up to her for fear of power. She portrayed herself as the oppressed, falsely accused one, when in reality, she was the slanderer and the transgressor.

www.ingramcontent.com/pod-product-compliance
Lightning Source LLC
LaVergne TN
LVHW052100160826
845678LV00015B/3300

* 9 7 8 1 7 3 8 5 4 1 3 0 0 *